KT-475-977

WINCHESTER SCHOOL OF MISSION

06093

Resource Room
Church House
9 The Close
WINCHESTER
SO23 9LS
Tel: 01962 624760

POCKET PRAYERS
FOR CHILDREN

POCKET PRAYERS
FOR CHILDREN

COMPILED BY
CHRISTOPHER HERBERT

CHURCH HOUSE
PUBLISHING

Church House Publishing
Church House
Great Smith Street
London SW1P 3NZ
Tel: 020 7898 1451
Fax: 020 7898 1449

ISBN 0 7151 4040 X

Published 1999 by The National Society and
Church House Publishing

Introduction and compilation copyright
© Christopher Herbert 1999 and 2004

This edition 2004

All rights reserved. No part of this publication may
be reproduced or stored or transmitted by any means
or in any form, electronic or mechanical, including
photocopying, recording, or any information storage
and retrieval system without written permission
which should be sought from the Copyright
Administrator, Church House Publishing, Church
House, Great Smith Street, London SW1P 3NZ
e-mail: copyright@c-of-e.org.uk.

Typeset by Vitaset, Paddock Wood, Kent
Printed in England by the University Printing Press,
Cambridge

Contents

FOR ROBIN AND KERRY
HERBERT WITH LOVE
AND ENORMOUS GRATITUDE

INTRODUCTION

I have very much enjoyed putting this collection of prayers together. You will see that there is a great variety here – some are very old and use traditional language, others are very new; some are written by children, others by famous people. What they all have in common is a desire to speak to God from the heart, with love and truth.

When the disciples of Jesus, almost two thousand years ago, asked him to teach them to pray, he replied with words that have become one of the most precious and treasured prayers in the world: the Lord's Prayer. This collection uses the phrases of the Lord's Prayer to provide a framework for each of the sections.

I hope that through using these prayers, but above all by using the Lord's Prayer, you will draw closer and closer to God and will come to know the depths of his love and his unending kindness and mercy.

+ Christopher Herbert
  Bishop of St Albans

How to use this book of prayers

The most important thing to realize when you pray is that God loves you. Prayer begins in his love and ends in his love. He wants us to come to him just as we are and talk to him in complete trust and honesty.

One of the best ways of praying is to find somewhere quiet and then be as still as you can for a few minutes, knowing that you are in the presence of God. Once you have become still, talk to God, either out loud or in the secret depths of your own heart, using your own words. Then you could turn to one or more of the prayers in this book to see if they can help you find the words for the things you also want to say. When you have said all your prayers, try being still again for a minute or two, just resting on God's love, and then end your prayers by saying the Lord's Prayer.

In this way you may establish a pattern for your prayers (silence; prayer in your own words; silence; the Lord's Prayer), which will be a real strength to you, not only now, but in the years that lie ahead.

Unless otherwise stated, all the prayers in this anthology were composed by Christopher Herbert.

THE LORD'S PRAYER

Our Father, who art in heaven,
hallowed be thy name;
thy kingdom come;
thy will be done;
on earth as it is in heaven.
Give us this day our daily bread.
And forgive us our trespasses,
as we forgive those who trespass
    against us.
And lead us not into temptation;
but deliver us from evil.

For thine is the kingdom,
    the power, and the glory,
for ever and ever. Amen.

*

CONTEMPORARY VERSION

Our Father in heaven,
hallowed be your name,
your kingdom come,
your will be done,
on earth as in heaven.
Give us today our daily bread.
Forgive us our sins
as we forgive those who sin against us.
Lead us not into temptation
but deliver us from evil.

For the kingdom, the power,
   and the glory are yours
now and for ever. Amen.

*

Our Father

There is not a single person,
not a single bird,
not a single blade of grass
which is outside your love, O Lord;
for you give life to everything,
and for your humility and power
we give you thanks and praise.

❋

God bless all those that I love;
God bless all those that love me;
God bless all those that love those
    that I love
and all those that love those that love me.

New England sampler

❋

Bless, O God, our families;
give to those who care for us
the spirit of understanding and the
    spirit of love
that our homes may be places of peace
    and of laughter
for Jesus' sake.

❋

Holy and loving God
open our eyes to see you,
open our minds to trust you;
open our hearts to love you
this day and for evermore.

❋

Thank you, God, for Kissy my dog when
    she was alive –
and letting me use her as a step to get
    onto the sofa.
Thank you, God, for my brother,
    Mackenzie.

Chelsea Pemberton Whiteley (age 6)

Lord God and heavenly Father,
you promised that you would come to us;
be with us in the silence of our hearts,
in the depths of our imagination,
at the centre of our lives,
and fill us with your love, now
      and for evermore.

*

Father, as those first shepherds knelt
      at the cradle,
      may we kneel quietly before you
just because we love you –
our most loving God and our most
      humble king.

*

Let all the world, O Lord,
come to know that you are our father,
our mother, our sister, our brother;
and through knowing you
may we then become
the family you would have us be,
for Jesus' sake.

O God, so beautiful;
O God, so holy;
O God, so loving
that you should die on a cross
for everyone and for me
is more than I can understand.
I come to you in the mystery of prayer
knowing that every day
you are bringing me closer
to your heart
and to your heaven,
through Jesus Christ, your Son, our Lord.

＊

In heaven

Alleluia! Praise the Lord from the heavens,
praise him in the heights.
Praise him, all you angels of his,
praise him, all you his host.
Praise him, sun and moon,
praise him, all you shining stars.
Praise him, heaven of heavens,
and you waters above the heavens.
Let them praise the name of the Lord,
for he commanded and they were created.
He made them stand fast for ever and ever,
he gave them a law which shall not
    pass away.
Praise the Lord from the earth,
you sea-monsters and all deeps;
Fire and hail, snow and fog,
tempestuous wind, doing his will;
Mountains and all hills,
fruit trees and all cedars;
Wild beasts and all cattle, creeping things
    and winged birds;
Kings of the earth and all peoples,
princes and all rulers of the world;

Young men and maidens,
old and young together.
Let them praise the name of the Lord,
for his name is exalted,
    his splendour is over earth and heaven.
He has raised up strength for his people
    and praise for all his loyal servants,
the children of Israel, a people who are
    near him. Alleluia!

Psalm 148: Celebrating Common Prayer

✳

Lord, you bathe the world with light;
bathe our hearts and our lives
with your peace, your love and your beauty
    for ever.

✳

When the sun is setting
and the sky changes colour very,
    very slowly
and with great beauty,
accept our quiet joy as a prayer of
thanksgiving to you,
our Lord and our God.

Lord,
the sun is full of energy
making seeds grow,
bringing us life.
Make us like the sun,
radiant with the glory of being alive
for Jesus' sake.

Lord God,
    you are the king of the universe,
king of creation
and king of glory; we worship you
    on this kingly day.

The light of Christ pierces the darkness
    like a sword;
the light of Christ engulfs the darkness
    like a fire;
the light of Christ conquers the darkness
    like a victorious army.
O light of Christ,
shine in our hearts and lives
and bring us your life and your
    eternal victory.

*

O most holy and most loving God,
surrounded by the songs of angels
and the laughter of saints,
grant us to know your presence
here on earth,
that we may enjoy you
now and for ever.

*

O king, all glorious –
shine into the depths of our hearts
with the brilliance of your love,
that our lives may be filled with the peace
of your most holy presence.

*

Glorious God,
radiant with light,
vibrant with love;
let our lives be so open to your presence
that we may share, even now,
in the joy and beauty of heaven,
for Jesus' sake.

*

HALLOWED BE YOUR NAME

God, you are our father and our mother,
    the life in all that exists;
thank you for the gift of your
    wonderful world,
for the gift of ourselves,
for the gift of other people
and for all whom we love.

*

Thank you, Lord, for all the rainbows
    of the world:
the rainbows in flowers,
the rainbows in streets,
the rainbows in traffic,
the rainbows in faces.
We praise and bless you, O holy God,
for a rainbow-full world.

*

Lord Jesus,
you are alive in our world:
alive in peals of laughter,
alive in the joy of love,
alive in the heart of music,
alive in the power of sunlight,
alive in the breath of life,
alive in the prayers
at the centre of our souls.
Lord Christ,
living Lord,
let us share in your most holy life,
now and for ever.

*

Dear God in heaven,
you are so beautiful,
so glorious,
so good,
that when I try to think about you
my mind reaches its very limits;
then all I can do is to thank you
    with all my heart
just because you are who you are.

Night is drawing nigh.
For all that has been – Thanks.
To all that shall be – *Yes*.

Dag Hammarskjöld 1905–61

*

Lord, we thy presence seek,
    May ours this blessing be;
Give us a pure and lowly heart,
A temple meet for thee.

John Keble 1792–1866

*

Glory to thee, my God, this night
    for all the blessings of the light;
keep me, O keep me, king of kings,
beneath thy own almighty wings.

Thomas Ken 1637–1711

*

Dear God,
I have stopped worrying about
    the bad things
and I've been thinking all about
    the good things in life
because I've been thinking about you.
Thank you. Amen.

Abigail Gouldbourne (age 7)

✳

God, you listen to me.
When I need help, you listen to me.
When I need comfort, you listen to me.
When I need guidance, you listen to me.
When I need love, you love me.

Becky Perrins (age 12)

✳

'I am': probably the most simple thing
    you said
but probably the most memorable.
It explains you so much –
how you said 'I am' to Moses from
    the burning bush
and everyone knew who you were,
that's because you're the only I am.

Kathryn Cockroft (age 12)

✱

When the day returns,
call us with morning faces,
    and with morning hearts,
eager to labour,
happy if happiness be our portion,
and if the day is marked for sorrow,
strong to endure.

Robert Louis Stevenson (1850–94)

✱

Lord, let thy glory be my end,
Thy word, my rule
and then thy will be done.

King Charles I (1600–48)

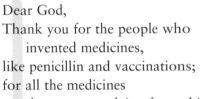

Dear God,
Thank you for the people who
    invented medicines,
like penicillin and vaccinations;
for all the medicines
    that stop you dying from things
like measles and smallpox and chickenpox.
Please allow people to make
    more medicines
until every single illness can be cured:
bacteria illnesses and virus illnesses.
I know you made all this amazing
    lovely universe
but I would like it if the dying rate could go
down very slowly, year by year. Amen.

Andrew Hood (age 6)

YOUR KINGDOM COME

Father, you have made the world
    very beautiful.
Teach us to love our world
and to treat it with reverence and with care
for Jesus' sake.

*

These are the patterns we have found:
lichen on a stone, cobwebs on hedgerows,
words on paper ...
Pattern our lives with your colours of love,
dear God,
that we may be beautiful for you.

*

We hold up to you, God, all the poor
   on the earth;
may we who are rich, share our wealth,
we who are well fed, share our food,
we who are educated, share our learning,
so that in our own small way
we may take part in the coming
   of your kingdom.

*

Lord, let your Holy Spirit rest upon
   our school
that it may be a place of love and truth,
where the weak are made strong
and the strong learn humility,
and all of us learn the wisdom
that alone comes from you.

*

Lord God,
let your peace rest so gently on our hearts
    and minds
that we may have the strength
to work for peace in our world,
today, tomorrow and for ever.

*

O God, our heavenly Father, whose Son,
our Lord Jesus Christ,
took the form of a servant and became
    the Man for others,
give us the same spirit of service
and help us to follow in his steps,
that with love and humility
we may give ourselves to those
    who need our help,
for the glory of your name.

Frank Colquhoun

*

Lord Jesus Christ
    risen from the tomb
your love is let loose in the world;
let your love conquer my heart
that I may become one of your disciples
and follow you for ever.

Lord, make me an instrument
    of your peace:
where there is hatred,
    let me bring your love;
where there is injury, pardon;
where there is discord, union;
where there is doubt, faith;
where there is despair, hope;
where there is darkness, light;
where there is sadness, joy;
for your mercy's sake.

Attributed to St Francis of Assisi (1182–1226)

Lord, you are love,
Lord, you are peace,
Lord, you are our gentle strength.
You are with us wherever we go
so we need not be afraid.
For your love, your peace
    and your strength
we thank you, now and always.

✳

YOUR WILL BE DONE, ON EARTH AS IN HEAVEN

When I wake up in the morning,
thank you, God, for being there.
When I go to school each day,
thank you, God, for being there.
When I am playing with my friends,
thank you, God, for being there.
And when I go to bed at night,
thank you, God, for being there.

✳

Almighty God, Father of all mankind,
in your Son, you took upon yourself
    the sorrow of the world.
We offer you our own sorrow and sadness,
knowing that you will help us
    to bear our grief
through the infinite understanding
    and love of Jesus Christ our Lord.

O God, I thank you
for all the creatures you have made,
so perfect in their kind –
great animals like the elephant
    and the rhinoceros,
humorous animals like the camel
    and the monkey,
friendly ones like the dog and the cat,
working ones like the horse and the ox,
timid ones like the squirrel and the rabbit,
majestic ones like the lion and the tiger,
for birds with their songs.
O Lord, give us such love
    for your creation
that love may cast out fear,
and all the creatures see in us
their priest and friend;
through Jesus Christ our Lord.

George Appleton (1902–93)

Lord Christ, shine upon all
who are in the darkness of suffering
   and grief,
that in your light, they may receive hope
   and courage
and in your presence, may find their rest
   and peace,
for your love's sake.

Alan Warren

There are some old people whose lives
   are like autumn:
mellow, quiet and wise.
Help us, Lord, to learn from them
and to listen to them patiently.

O loving Father,
I offer myself to be used by you
for the comforting of the sad,
the strengthening of the weak
and the befriending of the lonely,
through Jesus Christ, our Lord.

✳

Let all the world in every corner sing
My God and King!
The heavens are not too high,
his praise may thither fly.
The earth is not too low,
his praises there may grow.
Let all the world in every corner sing,
My God and King!

George Herbert (1593–1632)

✳

Christ has no body now on earth
    but yours,
no hands but yours, no feet but yours;
yours are the eyes
through which to look with Christ's
    compassion on the world,
yours are the feet
with which he is to go about doing good,
and yours are the hands
with which he is to bless us now.

St Teresa of Avila (1515–82)

Lord Jesus,
You suffered so much pain and cruelty
    on the cross
But through it all, you held on to love.
Be with us whenever life is very, very tough
and keep us loving, no matter
    what happens –
for that is your way,
the way that leads to peace and truth.

Dear God,
protect all the creatures of the world:
from the tiny money spider on his web
to the huge blue whale in the deep
        blue ocean,
from the gentle manatee in the Florida
        Everglades
to the fierce tiger in the Indian jungle,
from the slow sloth in the South American
        rain forest
to the speedy cheetahs on the African plain.
This world you have made, with all its
        different habitats,
is such a wonderful place.
Care for us and all the creatures
who share this beautiful world. Amen.

Matthew Swan (age 10)

*

Dear Lord,
Let kindness get to people's hearts
    like a raindrop
on a spider's web.
Let all the bad things, like drugs,
    get washed away by love.
Let all the young people grow up
    to be good
and honest, and help them not to lead
    a life of crime.
Lord, in your mercy,
hear my prayer.

Hannah Holt (age 9)

*

Dear God,
Look after everyone we love.
Help me with my tests this week.
Help me to get my Capitals in the
    right place.
Help Buttons, my dog, to be brave
    for his injections.
Amen.

Philip Lewis (age 7)

GIVE US TODAY OUR DAILY BREAD

Like a seagull gliding on the wind,
may we trust ourselves to your love,
   O Lord.

*

Blessed are you, Lord our God,
   king of the universe,
who feeds the entire world in his goodness –
with grace, with kindness and with mercy.
He gives food to all life, for his kindness
   is eternal ...
Blessed are you, God, who nourishes all.

Jewish Grace

*

The bread is pure and fresh,
the water is cool and clear.
Lord of all life, be with us.
Lord of all life, be near.

African Grace

God is great,
God is good,
let us thank him for this food.

Anon

*

God is with me now.
God sees me.
God hears me.
God smiles at me.
God loves me.
God wants me –
now and always.

From St Saviour's Priory

*

Lord, you are our hope and strength,
staying with us in trouble,
walking with us in danger
and comforting us in our sadness.
Keep us always mindful of your love
that we may be strong and courageous
in all that we think and speak and do,
knowing that you are our closest and most
    loyal friend.

Give us big hearts, dear God,
big enough to embrace everyone,
big enough to say sorry,
big enough to be humble,
big enough for you.

*

Eternal Light, shine into our hearts,
Eternal Goodness, deliver us from evil,
Eternal Power, be our support,
Eternal Wisdom, scatter the darkness of
    our ignorance,
Eternal Pity, have mercy on us;
that with all our heart and mind and soul
    and strength
we may seek your face and be brought by
    thine infinite mercy
to thy holy presence; through Jesus Christ
    our Lord.

Alcuin of York (AD 735–804)

*

Bless with your wisdom and patience,
dear God,
the farmers of the world,
that they may work with you
    and your creation
for the good of us all.

✳

Our prayer, dear Lord,
is that we shall do something to feed
    the hungry
and shall work for justice in our world,
through Jesus Christ our Lord.

✳

Bread is a lovely thing to eat –
God bless the barley and the wheat,
A lovely thing to breathe is air –
God bless the sunshine everywhere.
The earth's a lovely place to know –
God bless the folks that come and go!
Alive's a lovely thing to be –
giver of life – we say – bless thee.

Anon

Make us worthy, Lord,
To serve our fellow men throughout
   the world
who live and die in poverty and hunger.
Give them, through our hands, this day
   their daily bread,
and by our understanding love,
    give peace and joy.

Mother Teresa of Calcutta (1910–97)

＊

FORGIVE US OUR SINS

Lord, we hold up to you those people who
    are violent.
We don't want to pretend that we aren't
    violent at times;
so, Lord, here we are –
puzzled by others and puzzled by ourselves.
Please make sense of us and show us
the way of peace.

*

Hands who touched the leper,
touch my wounded heart;
hands who healed the blind man,
heal my aching soul;
hands who cured the lame,
mend my disjointed life;
hands who embraced all life,
enfold me in your peace.
Lord, merely touch and heal,
cure and forgive.

Anon

O Lord Jesus, we confess
that we are sometimes deliberately unkind
    to other people.
Forgive us and help us to show them
    your love.

❋

Heavenly Father,
    your light overcomes darkness;
take everything in my life that is dark
and transform it into glory;
through Jesus Christ our Lord.

❋

Peter promised that he would stay with you
    always, Lord,
and then he abandoned you
and felt ashamed.
I know that I might have done the same –
and so, as you forgave Peter,
giving him the courage
    to proclaim your resurrection,
forgive me when I abandon my friends
and give me the courage to say I'm sorry
to them and to you.

*

O God, full of love, hear my prayer.
If we have done things which shame us,
show us the right way.
Thank you for your love which surrounds
    us each day
and goes with us into the peace of night.

Anon

*

In the darkest moment of our lives, O God,
    remind us that you are light,
you are hope,
you are love.

＊

Dear God,
Why do I get cross when I lose my
    pocket money?
Why do I feel jealous when my friends get
    lots of presents?
Why do I get pleased when my sister gets
    told off?
Why do I feel sad when I have
    too many toys?
I hope you understand me, and I'm very,
    very sorry.
Amen.

Alice Taylor (age 8)

＊

Dear God,
Where did we go wrong?
What have we done to your
	wonderful world?
Why is it that some have plenty, while
	others have none?
Why do we start wars, killing lots of people?
What is the reason for birth and death?
What is the purpose of this place, this
	world, Earth?
Only you know these things. Amen.

Amanda Partridge (age 11)

*

Lamb of God, you take away the sins
	of the world:
have mercy on us.
Lamb of God, you take away the sins
	of the world:
have mercy on us.
Lamb of God, you take away the sins
	of the world:
grant us peace.

Ancient Greek Prayer

AS WE FORGIVE THOSE WHO SIN AGAINST US

When your friends betrayed you, Lord,
you took their sins upon yourself
and forgave them.
Please forgive us when we betray those
    we love
and when we betray you,
for without your forgiveness
our lives will become bitter and sad.
We are sorry, O God;
O God, please forgive.

*

Drop thy still dews of quietness,
till all our strivings cease;
take from our souls the strain and stress,
and let our ordered lives confess
the beauty of thy peace.

John Greenleaf Whittier (1807–1892)

Incline us, O God!
to think humbly of ourselves,
to be saved only in the examination of our
   own conduct,
to consider our fellow creatures
   with kindness,
and to judge of all they say and do
with the charity which we would desire
   from them ourselves.

Jane Austen (1775–1817)

Lord, increase our understanding
of ourselves, of each other, of you;
through the power of your Holy Spirit
and for the sake of your kingdom,
this day and always.

O Divine Master,
Grant that I may not so much seek
To be consoled, as to console,
To be understood, as to understand,
To be loved, as to love,
For it is in giving that we receive;
It is in pardoning
    that we are pardoned;
And it is in dying
    that we are born to eternal life.

St Francis of Assisi (1182–1226)

*

On that Good Friday, Lord,
they tried everything.
They tried to quench your love with insults,
to drown your love in jeering,
to kill your love
by nailing you to a cross.
But your love was not to be beaten.
You forgave them their insults,
you forgave them the jeering,
you forgave them the piercing;
and in your forgiveness
your love conquered all
and rose into new and eternal life.
For your ceaseless and most patient love
we give you thanks and praise,
our wounded and most holy Saviour.

*

Dear Lord,
    I would like to talk.
How do you become friends with someone
who doesn't like you particularly?
There is a girl in my class who likes all of
    my friends
but I get the impression she doesn't like me.
Should I feel hurt?
Should I talk to her?
Should I try to ignore it?
I don't know and I just thought
    you might know.
I know you will care and answer me.
    Amen.

Charlotte Dyer (age 9)

*

LEAD US NOT INTO TEMPTATION

Thank you, heavenly Father,
for those who risk their lives
in storms and great dangers
to bring others to safety.
When they are frightened, protect them;
when they are in peril, comfort them
and give them at all times
your peace and your strength,
 for Jesus' sake.

*

The sea sweeps up the beach
 and laps around the sandcastles
until they crumble and fall.
On the farther side of the beach,
near the cliff,
the sea dashes against the rocks
and they stand firm and strong.
Help us, at all times, O Lord,
to be more like the rock than sand.

The things, good Lord, that we pray for,
give us the grace to labour for.

Thomas More (1478–1535)

*

God give us grace to accept with serenity
    the things that cannot be changed,
courage to change the things that should
    be changed,
and the wisdom to distinguish the one
    from the other.

Reinhold Niebuhr (1892–1971)

*

Save us, O Lord, waking,
    and guard us, sleeping,
that awake we may watch with Christ
and asleep we may rest in peace.

From the Service of Compline

*

O Father in heaven,
when I am confused
and do not know what I should do,
give me, deep in my heart,
the knowledge I need,
and then the courage
to put that knowledge into action,
through Jesus Christ our Lord.

✳

Lord Jesus Christ,
when you were put to the final test
you did not flinch
but, with undaunted courage,
walked the way of the cross;
give us, we pray, the desire
and the courage
to follow your way of love,
each and every day,
for your name's sake.

✳

O God,
    you know me better than I know myself;
when I face temptation,
give me strength to overcome,
but if I fail,
be merciful, I pray,
for the sake of your Son,
Jesus Christ our Lord.

✳

BUT DELIVER US FROM EVIL

Almighty God,
who gave your only Son to die for the sins
    of the world;
have mercy on all who are tempted
and on all who, through weakness
    or wilfulness,
fall into sin;
reveal to them your gracious love,
that turning to you for help,
they may be led into fellowship with you
and obedience to your will;
through Jesus Christ our Lord.

*

Dear Father,
When I am scared
and I think monsters are going to come,
help me not to think that;
because I know they're not, if you are there.
Amen.

Wesley Wrigley (age 6)

Dear Lord Jesus,
help all those children who are in sadness
because of divorce with their parents.
Make them feel loved,
even without one of their parents,
by your love.
Bless the mothers and fathers as well;
make them realize
what is happening to their family. Amen.

Rebecca Toms (age 10)

*

Dear God,
I hope you can hear me,
lots of fighting and war is going on
    below you.
The thing I would really like to say is
help us to start again
and so this time we would know what
    would happen
if we destroy it and it will be
    a complete misery.
Help not just my family
but other families too who have split up.

Please help split up families (especially
    with children)
because I am in a very hard position
    at the moment
because my mum and dad have split up.

Sometimes I think to myself
it seems that me and my sister are right
    stuck in the middle and I can't get out.
Please help us to create peace
and to love and care.

I expect you are feeling very sad;
I would help if I could
but I am only one person
    out of thousands of people
and it would be hard
    to let everybody know;
so I just can't help.
I'll have to go now, speak to you later.

A young girl (age 8)

*

I bind unto myself today
the power of God to hold and lead,
his eye to watch, his might to stay,
his ear to hearken to my need;
the wisdom of my God to teach,
his hand to guide, his shield to ward,
the word of God to give me speech,
his heavenly host to be my guard.

St Patrick (389–461)

*

Dear Lord,
I would just like to say what
        a changing place
the world is starting to be.
Ever since the Dunblane incident,
        for example,
I, and many others, have become worried
        and shaky
about lots of things.
Whenever I'm on my own, I feel insecure,
and if a parent or guardian isn't there
to pick me up when I've finished
        an activity,
I start to worry.
I would just love it if there was nothing
to worry about in the world.
So please, God, help me
and everyone else
to stay confident and not to worry;
through Jesus' name. Amen.

Matthew Neville (age 11)

Father in heaven,
when the darkness threatens
    to overwhelm us
and we are very afraid,
be with us in your love,
and banish from our hearts and minds
all the terrors and evil of the world,
and then enfold us in your peace,
for Jesus' sake.

*

FOR THE KINGDOM

Lord in heaven, you have promised us new life
through your Son, Jesus Christ;
help us to live with that promise
in our hearts and in our lives,
so that our sadness can be turned by you
into blessing and strength in the days ahead.

*

Dear Lord,
thank you for football,
for the fun of it:
slide tackles, overhead kicks,
and diving and long shots;
for the skill of it:
passing accurately,
dribbling, kick ups and volleys;
for the joy of it
when you score a goal.
Good football is excellent.
Thank you, God, for football.

Shaun Kemp (age 8)

In the silence
    The deep, echoing silence
I listen for You.

In the dark
The calm, tranquil dark
I listen for You.

In the storm
The howling, raging storm
I listen for You.

In the waves
The crashing, ravening waves
I listen for You.

By the stream,
The tumbling, bubbling stream
I listen for You.

In the woods
The cool, shady woods
I listen for You.

And in the calm and the quiet
The power and the noise
The serene and the busy
I listen
And You are there.

Frances James (age 12)

O holy God, you have made our world
    very curious;
help me, as I explore your world,
to discover your presence in all things,
for Jesus' sake.

*

Be thou my vision, O Lord of my heart,
Be all else but naught to me,
    save that thou art,
Be thou my best thought in the day
    and the night,
Both waking and sleeping,
    thy presence my light.

Traditional Irish hymn

*

Eternal God and Father,
by whose power we are created
and by whose love we are redeemed,
guide and strengthen us by your Spirit,
that we may give ourselves to your service
and live in love to one another and to you,
through Jesus Christ our Lord.

Joint Liturgical Group

✳

O most loving God,
you are at the very centre of all life
and embrace the universe with your love;
open our eyes to see you,
our minds to know you,
and our hearts to love you –
this day, and for evermore.

✳

THE POWER

Morning glory, starlit sky,
Leaves in springtime, swallows' flight,
Autumn gales, tremendous seas,
Sounds and scents of summer night;

Soaring music, tow'ring words,
Art's perfection, scholar's truth,
Joy supreme of human love,
Memory's treasure, grace of youth;

Open, Lord, are these, Thy gifts,
Gifts of love to mind and sense;
Hidden is love's agony,
Love's endeavour, love's expense.

Love that gives, gives ever more,
Gives with zeal, with eager hands,
Spares not, keeps not, all outpours,
Ventures all, its all expends.

Drained is love in making full;
Bound in setting others free;
Poor in making many rich;
Weak in giving power to be.

Therefore He Who Thee reveals
Hangs, O Father, on that Tree
Helpless; and the nails and thorns
Tell of what Thy love must be.

Thou art God; no monarch Thou
Thron'd in easy state to reign;
Thou art God, Whose arms of love
Aching, spent, the world sustain.

W. H. Vanstone

✳

The water comes crashing down
    the mountain,
turning waterwheels, driving turbines,
giving us energy for our work and our play.
Come to us, O Lord, in your power
and fill our lives with the energy
    of your Holy Spirit
that we may bring life to others.

✳

Dear God,
thank you for my happy life.
Amen.

Olivia Powell (age 4)

﹡

Dear Father God,
thank you for making me.
I can dance and I can run.

Amy Dale (age 5)

﹡

Ah, the fragrance of new grass!
I hear his footsteps coming –
the Lord of the resurrection.

Jiro Sasaki, Bishop of Kyoto

﹡

All your works praise you, O Lord,
and your faithful servants bless you.
They make known the glory of
   your kingdom
and speak of your power;
That the peoples may know of your power
and the glorious splendour of
   your kingdom.
Your kingdom is an everlasting kingdom,
your dominion endures throughout all ages.
The Lord is faithful in all his words
and merciful in all his deeds.
The Lord upholds all those who are
   bowed down.
The eyes of all await upon you, O Lord,
and you give them their food in
   due season.

Psalm 145.10–16: Celebrating Common Prayer

Be still, for the presence of the Lord, the
    Holy One, is here;
come, bow before him now, with reverence
    and fear.
In him no sin is found, we stand
    on holy ground.
Be still, for the presence of the Lord, the
    Holy One, is here.

Be still, for the glory of the Lord is shining
    all around;
he burns with holy fire, with splendour he
    is crowned.
How awesome is the sight, our radiant
    King of Light!
Be still, for the glory of the Lord is shining
    all around.

Be still, for the power of the Lord is
    moving in this place,
he comes to cleanse and heal, to minister
    his grace.
No work too hard for him, in faith receive
    from him;
be still, for the power of the Lord is moving
    in this place.

David J. Evans (b.1957)

... AND THE GLORY
ARE YOURS

Mountains are very still,
they just sit and sit.
They point to your greatness, O God,
silent and quiet.
Help me to be still and silent,
like a mountain;
sitting still, listening to your voice.

Timothy King

✳

O God, Creator of Light,
at the rising of your sun this morning,
let the greatest of all lights,
your love,
rise like the sun within our hearts.

Prayer of the Armenian Apostolic Church

✳

Father of love,
    make us like gleaming mirrors
so that we may reflect your glorious light.

*

In the soaring beauty of our cathedrals,
    O God,
let your simple presence dwell,
that we may come close to you in holiness
and in your holiness, find our peace;
for Jesus' sake.

*

Dear Lord,
I pray for all those people who are scared
    of the dark
and feel darkness inside them.
Please help them to battle through
    the nothingness
of the night.
It is lonely in the dark
and people sometimes don't feel
    your presence.
Please help those people
to feel that you are there.
When we are scared
please help us.
Thank your for helping us
by giving us the gift of life.
You are the light of the world.
Help us see, Lord. Amen.

Christopher Clayton (age 10)

﹡

Lord,
make me like a mirror
facing the place where the sun
    always shines,
so I can reflect the joy of the sun
on to all of the people.

Lauren Newman (age 8)

*

Now and for ever.
Amen.

When words fail me, Lord,
 and I don't know what to make
 of things,
help me to be really silent,
 deep-down silent,
and wait in trust for the answers.

※

Alone with none but thee, my God,
I journey on my way.
What need I fear when thou art near
O king of night and day?
More safe am I within thy hand
than if a host did round me stand.

St Columba (AD 521–97)

※

Draw us nearer to you each day,
O Lord,
for you are our purpose and
our destiny.

May the road rise to meet you.
May the wind always be at your back.
May the sun shine warm upon your face,
the rain fall soft upon your fields,
and until we meet again,
may God hold you in the palm of
his hand.

Traditional Celtic blessing

O Father, all time is in your hands.
May we hold on to that which is good
    from the past,
to be aware of the joys of the present
and rejoice in the endless promise
    of the future.

＊

I know, O God,
that wherever I travel,
you will be with me.
There is nowhere I can go,
nothing I can face
which is beyond your love and strength.
And so I place myself
into your care and keeping,
knowing that at all times
and in all places,
I am in your hands.

＊

Word of God, give me the words
    To praise you for ever and ever.

*

Jesus Christ, thou child so wise
Bless mine hands and fill mine eyes
And bring my soul to Paradise.

Hilaire Belloc

*

Be thou a bright flame before me,
Be thou a guiding star above me,
Be thou a smooth path below me
And a kindly shepherd behind me,
Today – tonight – and for ever.

St Columba (AD 521–97)

*

The Lord bless us and keep us,
the Lord make his face to shine
    upon us,
and be gracious unto us;
the Lord lift up the light of his countenance
    upon us,
and give us peace.

Traditional blessing, based on Numbers 6.24-6

✳

God, let your blessing rest upon us
like dew on the grass,
bringing refreshment, beauty and peace
to body, mind and soul.

✳

Lord, keep us safe this night,
secure from all our fears.
May angels guard us while we sleep
till morning light appears.

Anon

*

God be in my head,
    and in my understanding;
God be in my eyes, and in my looking;
God be in my mouth, and in my speaking;
God be in my heart, and in my thinking;
God be at my end, and at my departing.

The Sarum Primer 1558

*

INDEX OF FIRST LINES

INDEX OF AUTHORS AND SOURCES

Acknowledgements

The author and publisher gratefully acknowledge permission to reproduce copyright material in this publication. Every effort has been made to trace and contact copyright holders. If there are any inadvertent omissions we apologise to those concerned and will ensure that a suitable acknowledgement is made at the next reprint.

The Archbishops' Council: The Lord's Prayer (modified traditional version) from *Common Worship* is reproduced by permission. The Lord's Prayer in its modern form is adapted from the International Consultation on English Texts (ICET) version (pp. 1–2).
The European Province of the Society of St Francis: Psalms 145 (p. 62) and 148 (p. 8) from *Celebrating Common Prayer*, 1992.
Faber & Faber Ltd: 'Dear God in heaven' from Dag Hammarsköld, *Markings*, 1964 (p. 13).
Joint Liturgical Group: 'Eternal God and Father' (p. 58).
Kingsway's Thankyou Music: 'Be still, for the presence of the Lord' by David J. Evans. Copyright © 1986 Kingsway's Thankyou Music. PO Box 75, Eastbourne, East Sussex BN23 6NW, UK. Used by kind permission (p. 63).

Mowbray, an imprint of Cassell plc: 'O God, our heavenly Father' by Frank Colquhoun (p. 20); 'Lord Christ, shine upon all' by Alan Warren (p. 25) from David Silk, *Prayers for Use at the Alternative Services*, 1980, 1986.

Oxford University Press: 'O God, I thank you' by George Appleton from *The Oxford Book of Prayer*, 1985 (p. 24).

SPCK: 'Make us worthy, Lord' by Mother Teresa of Calcutta from Robert Runcie and Basil Hume, *Prayers for Peace*, 1987 (p. 34).

W. H. Vanstone: 'Morning glory, starlit night', copyright © James William Shore, from W. H. Vanstone, *Love's Endeavour, Love's Expense*, Darton, Longman & Todd, 1977 (p. 59).

Prayers by Christopher Clayton (p. 66), Kathryn Cockroft (p. 16), Amy Dale (p. 61), Charlotte Dyer (p. 44), Abigail Gouldbourne (p. 15), Hannah Holt (p. 29), Andrew Hood (p. 17), Frances James (p. 56), Shaun Kemp (p. 55), Philip Lewis (p. 29), Matthew Neville (p. 53), Lauren Newman (p. 67), Amanda Partridge (p. 39), Becky Perrins (p. 15), Olivia Powell (p. 61), Matthew Swan (p. 28), Alice Taylor (p. 38), Rebecca Toms (p. 50), Chelsea Pemberton Whiteley (p. 4), Wesley Wrigley (p. 49), and A young girl (p. 51) are prize-winning entries of the 1998 *Together for Children* prayer competition and are reproduced by permission.

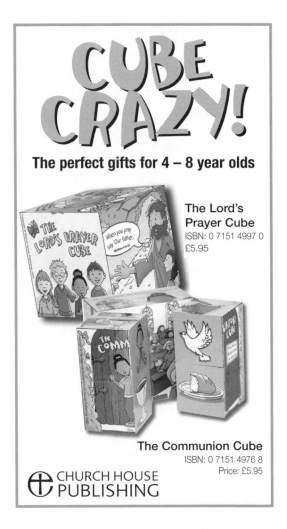

CUBE CRAZY!

The perfect gifts for 4 – 8 year olds

The Lord's Prayer Cube
ISBN: 0 7151 4997 0
£5.95

The Communion Cube
ISBN: 0 7151 4976 8
Price: £5.95

CHURCH HOUSE
PUBLISHING

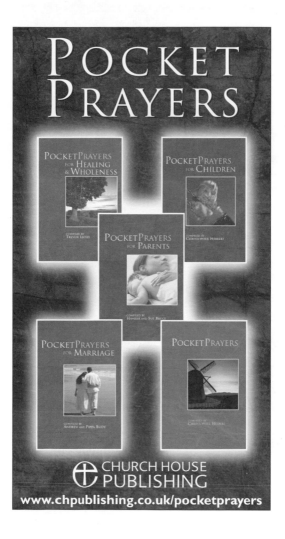